It Could Still Be A Dinosaur

By Allan Fowler

Consultants:
Robert L. Hillerich, Professor Emeritus,
Bowling Green State University, Bowling Green, Ohio
Consultant, Pinellas County Schools, Florida

Lynn Kepler, Educational Consultant

Fay Robinson, Child Development Specialist

CHILDRENS PRESS®
CHICAGO

Design by Beth Herman Design Associates

Library of Congress Cataloging-in-Publication Data

Fowler, Allan.
　　It could still be a dinosaur / by Allan Fowler.
　　　　p. cm. – (Rookie read-about science)
　　Summary: Illustrations and brief text describe some of the different
dinosaurs that lived millions of years ago.
　　ISBN 0-516-06002-3
　　1. Dinosaurs–Juvenile literature. [1. Dinosaurs.] I. Title.
　II. Series: Fowler, Allan. Rookie read-about science.
QE862.D5F69 1992
567.9'1–dc20   92-9411
　　　　　　　　　　　　　　　　　　　　　　　　　　CIP
　　　　　　　　　　　　　　　　　　　　　　　　　　AC

It's a dinosaur! But you
knew that, didn't you?

You may also know its name – Apatosaurus.

It used to be called Brontosaurus.

Scientists thought that Apatosaurus and Brontosaurus were different dinosaurs.

But when enough bones had
been dug up and compared,
the scientists knew they had
made a mistake.

Apatosaurus and Brontosaurus
were the same animal. And
Apatosaurus is the only name
they call it by now.

A dinosaur could have been almost any shape or size.

It could have had a bill
like a duck – and still
have been a dinosaur.

This Corythosaurus...

and this Diplodocus, and the
Apatosaurus, ate only plants.

But an animal could
have eaten meat –

and still have been
a dinosaur.

Tyrannosaurus was so fierce –
look at those sharp teeth! –
that it even ate other dinosaurs.

An animal could have been smaller than a turkey, like this Coelophysis bauri,

or it could have weighed as much as fifteen elephants, like Brachiosaurus – and still have been a dinosaur.

It could have had plates on
its back, like Stegosaurus...

or horns on its head,
like Triceratops...

or been covered with thick
armor, like Ankylosaurus –
and still have been a
dinosaur.

Where can you see a
dinosaur today?

You might find a skeleton
or a model of a dinosaur in
a museum.

23

But all the dinosaurs – except
for one small kind – died out
millions of years ago.

That was a long, long time
before there were any
people on Earth.

The only kind of dinosaur that didn't vanish looked like this. It had wings and feathers.

It was called Archaeopteryx.

And it kept changing over the years until it became the first bird.

27

Does that mean a chicken
or a robin or a seagull is
really a dinosaur?

Well, you could say it is –
in a way!

Words You Know

Apatosaurus

Triceratops

Archaeopteryx

Stegosaurus

skeleton/museum

Brachiosaurus

Tyrannosaurus

Ankylosaurus

Diplodocus

Index

About the Author

Allan Fowler is a free-lance writer with a background in advertising. Born in New York, he lives in Chicago now and enjoys traveling.

Photo Credits

Transparency #2417 by Charles R. Knight, Courtesy Department of Library Services, American Museum of Natural History – 5

Neg #36246, Courtesy Department of Library Services, American Museum of Natural History – 6-7

Dinosaur National Monument – 18, 30 (bottom right)

©Brian Franczak – 15, 17, 24-25, 31 (center left)

The Natural History Museum, London – #S04547/D 20, 31 (bottom left); #T01213/F 27, 30 (bottom left)

©David Peters – Cover, 9

PhotoEdit – ©John Neubauer, 23, 31 (top)

SuperStock International, Inc. – 8, 10, 11, 12-13, 31 (bottom right and center right)

Valan – ©Harold V. Green, 3, 30 (top left); ©Pam E. Hickman, 14, 19, 30 (top right); ©John Cancalosi, 29

COVER: Brachiosaurus